PRINCEWILL LAGANG

Marriage Matters: Christian Wisdom for Couples

First published by PRINCEWILL LAGANG 2023

Copyright © 2023 by Princewill Lagang

All rights reserved. No part of this publication may be reproduced, stored or transmitted in any form or by any means, electronic, mechanical, photocopying, recording, scanning, or otherwise without written permission from the publisher. It is illegal to copy this book, post it to a website, or distribute it by any other means without permission.

Princewill Lagang asserts the moral right to be identified as the author of this work.

First edition

This book was professionally typeset on Reedsy.
Find out more at reedsy.com

Contents

1	The Foundation of Love	1
2	Love in Action	4
3	The Art of Communication	7
4	The Sanctity of Intimacy	10
5	Family and Faith	13
6	Navigating Challenges Together	16
7	A Life of Purpose	19
8	Cherishing the Journey	22
9	Sustaining Hope	25
10	The Legacy of Love	28
11	Book Summary: Marriage Matters: Christian Wisdom for Couples	31

1

The Foundation of Love

Marriage Matters: Christian Wisdom for Couples

As the morning sun cast its gentle glow upon the quaint village of St. Augustine, a small chapel nestled amidst the rolling hills stood as a beacon of hope and commitment. The clear skies seemed to bless this sacred place, where two souls would soon unite in holy matrimony. Inside, the pews filled with family and friends, awaiting the arrival of the bride and groom.

In a world of shifting values and ever-changing norms, the institution of marriage remains a cornerstone of Christian faith. It is not only a legal union but a spiritual covenant. This book, "Marriage Matters: Christian Wisdom for Couples," embarks on a journey to explore the profound, ageless wisdom that Christianity offers to couples as they prepare to embark on a lifelong commitment. It is a call to understand that marriage, in the Christian tradition, is not just about the union of two individuals but the intertwining of two souls.

The Divine Blueprint for Love

Marriage, as we know it today, finds its roots in the ancient biblical traditions. It is an institution that was sanctified by God Himself, dating back to the book of Genesis. In Genesis 2:24, we read the following words: "Therefore a man shall leave his father and mother and be joined to his wife, and they shall become one flesh." These words, spoken by God, are the cornerstone of Christian marriage. It is a profound statement that captures the essence of the union: two individuals coming together to form a single, harmonious entity.

In a world often marred by individualism and fleeting relationships, the notion of becoming "one flesh" stands as a powerful testament to the divine blueprint for love and companionship. It speaks to the profound unity that marriage represents, where two distinct personalities blend together in an intricate dance of love and commitment.

The Sanctity of Marriage

Marriage is not a social contract; it is a sacred covenant. In Christian theology, the act of marriage is considered a sacrament, a tangible and visible sign of God's grace. This recognition of marriage's holiness underlines its significance, as it draws couples closer to the Divine and challenges them to exemplify the love and devotion that Christ showed to His Church.

The solemn commitment in marriage echoes the covenant between God and His people. In this covenant, God promises unwavering love, and in return, the people pledge their devotion. Similarly, in the Christian marriage covenant, couples promise to love, honor, and cherish one another, in good times and bad, in sickness and in health, forsaking all others until death. This unwavering commitment, mirroring God's faithfulness, is what elevates marriage to a sacred institution in the Christian faith.

Embracing the Journey

"Marriage Matters: Christian Wisdom for Couples" is a journey that traverses through the depths of Christian teachings, unveiling the timeless wisdom and guidance that Christianity offers to couples on their matrimonial voyage. We will explore the virtues of love, patience, and forgiveness that are rooted in Christian tradition, and we will delve into the spiritual practices that can strengthen the marital bond.

Throughout this book, we will draw from the wisdom of theologians, pastors, and couples who have walked the path of Christian matrimony. We will reflect on the power of prayer, the significance of mutual respect, and the joy of companionship as we aim to unlock the secrets to a thriving Christian marriage.

So, as we begin this journey together, let us remember that marriage, when guided by Christian wisdom, can be a source of profound joy, spiritual growth, and a testament to the divine love that knows no bounds. Let's embark on this exploration of "Marriage Matters: Christian Wisdom for Couples," with open hearts and a commitment to building strong, lasting, and God-centered unions.

2

Love in Action

Marriage Matters: Christian Wisdom for Couples

The gentle rays of the morning sun bathed the small village chapel in a golden glow, reminiscent of the love that had blossomed within its walls. Inside, the newlyweds, Sarah and Michael, knelt before the altar, their hands clasped together in prayer, marking the beginning of their lifelong journey as husband and wife.

In the previous chapter, we explored the sacred foundation of Christian marriage, emphasizing its divine nature and the profound covenant it forms between two souls. This chapter, titled "Love in Action," delves into the heart of Christian matrimony - love. In the Christian faith, love is not merely a feeling but a continuous, intentional choice and action.

Agape Love: A Divine Model

In the Greek language, there are several words for love, and agape is a term that holds a special place in Christian theology. Agape love is the unconditional, sacrificial love that reflects God's love for humanity. It is a love that seeks the well-being of the other above all else, even when it demands personal sacrifice.

In the Christian marriage context, agape love serves as the bedrock. It is the love that remains unwavering through trials and tribulations, a love that acts selflessly even when the emotions waver. As the Apostle Paul wrote in 1 Corinthians 13:4-7: "Love is patient, love is kind. It does not envy, it does not boast, it is not proud. It does not dishonor others, it is not self-seeking, it is not easily angered, it keeps no record of wrongs. Love does not delight in evil but rejoices with the truth. It always protects, always trusts, always hopes, always perseveres."

The Power of Forgiveness

No marriage is without its share of conflicts and misunderstandings. However, the Christian marriage is distinguished by the emphasis on forgiveness as an essential practice. Christ's teaching on forgiveness, as exemplified in the Lord's Prayer, calls for us to forgive others as God forgives us.

Forgiveness in marriage is not just about saying the words but embodying them through actions. It means letting go of grudges, extending grace, and seeking reconciliation. In forgiveness, we mirror the divine love of Christ, who forgave us of our sins.

Love Languages

Understanding how you and your spouse give and receive love is a crucial aspect of Christian marriage. Dr. Gary Chapman's concept of "love languages" helps couples recognize and appreciate the unique ways in which they express and interpret love. The five primary love languages are words of affirmation, acts of service, receiving gifts, quality time, and physical touch.

By discovering your spouse's love language and actively engaging with it, you show love in a manner that resonates with them. This practice creates a deeper sense of connection and intimacy within the marriage, aligning with the Christian principle of putting the other's needs above your own.

Growing Together in Love

"Love in Action" is not a mere theoretical concept; it is the daily practice of choosing to love your spouse as Christ loves the Church. It is the commitment to agape love, the willingness to forgive, and the exploration of each other's love languages. In this chapter, we've touched upon the practical foundations of Christian love in marriage, but the journey continues.

As we move forward in this exploration of "Marriage Matters: Christian Wisdom for Couples," remember that love is not a mere sentiment but a steadfast commitment. It is a decision to act, to choose love even when the emotions ebb and flow. By embracing this profound understanding of love, you can transform your marriage into a living testament of God's love for His people, a beacon of light that shines brightly in a world longing for authentic, sacrificial love.

3

The Art of Communication

Marriage Matters: Christian Wisdom for Couples

The morning sun painted a serene portrait as it peeked through the curtains of Sarah and Michael's home. In this sacred space, they were beginning another day of their journey as a married couple. The aroma of freshly brewed coffee filled the air, mingling with the sound of their laughter as they shared their thoughts and dreams, reflecting a marriage grounded in open, honest, and heartfelt communication.

In this chapter, titled "The Art of Communication," we dive into one of the most critical aspects of a successful and God-centered marriage. Effective communication is not just about speaking and listening but is a profound tool for understanding, resolving conflicts, and growing together in love.

Listening with Compassion

A fundamental Christian teaching that is often overlooked in the realm of communication is the art of listening with compassion. In the book of James, we are reminded to be "quick to listen, slow to speak, and slow to become angry." Listening with compassion is an expression of love, respect, and empathy for your spouse's thoughts and feelings.

To truly listen, set aside distractions, provide your full attention, and be open to your partner's words, no matter how difficult or joyous they may be. Listening with compassion allows you to understand your spouse on a deeper level and nurtures a sense of trust and intimacy.

Words that Build Up

The Bible is replete with wisdom about the power of our words. In Proverbs 18:21, it is said, "The tongue has the power of life and death." As such, we must be mindful of the words we use when communicating with our spouses. Our words can either breathe life into our relationship or cause harm. They can affirm, encourage, and inspire, or they can wound, demean, and destroy.

The Christian call to communication is to use words that build up, words that reflect God's grace and love. Practice speaking words of love, kindness, and affirmation, and avoid words that can lead to discord or misunderstanding. Encourage each other to speak the truth with love and gentleness, guided by the principle found in Ephesians 4:29: "Do not let any unwholesome talk come out of your mouths, but only what is helpful for building others up according to their needs, that it may benefit those who listen."

Conflict Resolution with Grace

No marriage is without its share of conflicts and disagreements. However, how a couple handles these moments is what truly matters. In the Christian marriage, conflict resolution is a journey guided by grace. It is about seeking resolution, not victory, and maintaining the love and respect for your spouse even in the midst of strife.

The Bible instructs us in Matthew 18:15-17 about addressing issues with a fellow believer, and these principles can be applied to marital conflicts.

The steps involve addressing the issue privately, seeking counsel from wise individuals, and, when necessary, involving the church community. The goal is to seek reconciliation and healing, adhering to the call for love and forgiveness.

Growing Through Dialogue

Effective communication is a means of growing together in love. As we delve into the art of communication, let us remember that it's not just about words but about understanding, empathy, and patience. It's about nurturing the bond between husband and wife, allowing it to thrive and flourish in the light of God's love.

In the ongoing journey of "Marriage Matters: Christian Wisdom for Couples," let the art of communication be a bridge that brings you closer to your spouse, enables you to resolve conflicts with grace, and helps you to continually grow together in the love that mirrors Christ's love for His Church. Embrace communication as a sacred practice, a vessel through which you express your love, seek understanding, and manifest the divine wisdom that guides your marriage.

4

The Sanctity of Intimacy

Marriage Matters: Christian Wisdom for Couples

As the sun dipped below the horizon, Sarah and Michael sat side by side, gazing out at the starlit sky from their cozy porch. In the warmth of their embrace, they felt a profound connection, transcending the physical world and touching their souls. This moment was a testament to the sacred nature of intimacy within a Christian marriage. In this chapter, "The Sanctity of Intimacy," we explore the profound spiritual and physical union that lies at the heart of marital intimacy.

Intimacy as a Gift from God

The Christian perspective on intimacy begins with the belief that God designed it as a beautiful and sacred gift. The Bible makes it clear in Genesis 2:24 that "a man shall leave his father and mother and be joined to his wife, and they shall become one flesh." This intimate joining of husband and wife is not only a physical act but a profound spiritual one. It mirrors the deep union between Christ and His Church, highlighting the sanctity of marital intimacy.

In a world that often commodifies and cheapens the concept of intimacy, the Christian approach places it on a pedestal, emphasizing its significance in the context of marriage. Intimacy is not just about satisfying physical desires; it is about deepening the bond between spouses and growing closer to God through the shared experience.

Mutual Submission and Respect

Ephesians 5:21-33 offers profound guidance on the dynamics of marital intimacy. It instructs husbands to love their wives as Christ loved the Church and wives to submit to their husbands. However, this submission is not about subservience but mutual respect and a willingness to honor and serve each other.

In the Christian marriage, intimacy is not a one-sided affair but a partnership. It involves a deep respect for each other's bodies, desires, and boundaries. It is about prioritizing your spouse's well-being and finding joy in selfless giving. This mutual submission and respect become the foundation for a healthy and fulfilling intimate life within the marital covenant.

Nurturing Emotional Intimacy

Intimacy goes beyond the physical realm; it extends to emotional closeness as well. To cultivate deep emotional intimacy, couples must create an environment of trust, vulnerability, and understanding. This entails active listening, empathetic communication, and a willingness to share one's deepest thoughts and feelings.

In the context of Christian marriage, nurturing emotional intimacy means allowing your spouse to see your true self, including your weaknesses and imperfections. This level of openness and vulnerability strengthens the marital bond and reflects the unconditional love and acceptance modeled by Christ.

A Reflection of God's Love

The sanctity of intimacy within a Christian marriage serves as a reflection of God's love. Just as Christ's love for His Church is deep and unwavering, so should be the love shared between husband and wife. The physical and spiritual union in intimacy becomes a tangible expression of that divine love, nurturing the connection between spouses and fostering an atmosphere of trust and safety.

As we explore "The Sanctity of Intimacy" in "Marriage Matters: Christian Wisdom for Couples," let us remember that intimacy is not a taboo subject but a vital part of a thriving marriage. It is a sacred gift from God that allows couples to experience His love in a unique and profound way. By embracing this divine gift and nurturing intimacy within the boundaries of the marital covenant, you not only honor your spouse but also honor God's design for a fulfilling and joy-filled marriage.

5

Family and Faith

Marriage Matters: Christian Wisdom for Couples

As Sarah and Michael stood together, hands in hand, in the soft morning light, they gazed upon their children playing in the garden, a testament to their love and commitment as a family. In this chapter, "Family and Faith," we delve into the profound role that family plays in Christian marriage and the ways in which faith enriches the experience of building a family.

The Family as a Divine Institution

The Christian perspective on family is rooted in the belief that the family is a divine institution. It is the fundamental building block of society and a vital component of God's plan for humanity. In the Bible, we find numerous references to family, from Adam and Eve in the garden to the Holy Family of Mary, Joseph, and Jesus.

Christian marriage is not just about the union of two individuals but the creation of a new family unit. It is an opportunity to fulfill the divine commandment to "be fruitful and multiply." Through family, we participate in God's creation, nurturing and raising the next generation in His love and teachings.

The Role of Parents as Stewards of Faith

Within the family, parents have a sacred role as stewards of faith. The responsibility to instill Christian values and beliefs in their children is a profound one. In Deuteronomy 6:6-7, parents are encouraged to "impress [God's commandments] on your children. Talk about them when you sit at home and when you walk along the road, when you lie down and when you get up."

This practice of imparting faith is not limited to religious instruction alone but extends to living out the Christian life as an example. Parents, through their actions and interactions, teach their children about love, forgiveness, and compassion, mirroring the love of Christ. The family serves as a sanctuary where children can learn to walk in the light of faith.

Challenges and Blessings of Family Life

While family life is a source of great joy, it also presents challenges. In the hustle and bustle of daily life, parents can struggle to find time for spiritual and family activities. Balancing work, school, extracurricular activities, and other responsibilities can be daunting.

However, Christian wisdom offers guidance on prioritizing faith within the family. Regular family prayer, reading the Bible, and participating in church activities can help keep faith at the forefront of family life. These practices not only strengthen the spiritual bond between family members but also provide a sense of grounding and stability in an ever-changing world.

The Legacy of Faith

In a Christian marriage, the legacy of faith is a precious gift that parents pass on to their children. It is an inheritance that far surpasses material possessions. By nurturing a deep, abiding faith within the family, parents provide their children with a moral compass and a source of strength to navigate the challenges of life.

"The Family and Faith" chapter of "Marriage Matters: Christian Wisdom for Couples" reminds us that the family unit, founded on the principles of love, faith, and togetherness, is a cornerstone of Christian life. It is within the family that faith is nurtured, values are instilled, and love is experienced, reflecting the profound love that God has for His children. As you continue your journey in a Christian marriage, may your family be a source of spiritual growth, joy, and a living testament to the love of Christ.

6

Navigating Challenges Together

Marriage Matters: Christian Wisdom for Couples

The peaceful serenity of Sarah and Michael's life was once again interrupted by the storms of life, and this time it was a financial crisis. In their journey through Christian marriage, they had encountered various trials, and this chapter, "Navigating Challenges Together," explores the profound wisdom that the Christian faith provides for couples facing adversity.

The Inevitability of Trials

The Christian perspective on marriage acknowledges that challenges are an inevitable part of life. In John 16:33, Jesus reassures his followers, saying, "In this world, you will have trouble. But take heart! I have overcome the world." This acknowledgment of trials and tribulations in life extends to marriage, where couples may face financial difficulties, health issues, or conflicts that test the strength of their bond.

Understanding that challenges are a natural part of life helps couples approach adversity with faith, resilience, and a united front. When difficulties arise, it is an opportunity for growth, both individually and as a couple.

Faith as an Anchor

The Christian faith serves as an anchor in the storms of life. It provides a source of strength, comfort, and hope in times of trouble. In Hebrews 6:19, faith is described as "an anchor for the soul, firm and secure."

Couples who rely on their faith can weather the storms of life more effectively. They find solace in prayer, seeking God's guidance and trusting in His plan. They can also lean on their church community for support and encouragement, further solidifying their bond and providing a lifeline during challenging times.

Practicing Patience and Forgiveness

In the face of trials, patience and forgiveness become vital virtues. It is important to remember that, as humans, we are imperfect and may make mistakes. We must extend grace to our spouse when they falter and seek forgiveness when we err.

Patience, often described in Galatians 5:22 as a fruit of the Spirit, allows us to approach difficulties with a calm and understanding heart. It is the ability to bear with one another's burdens and imperfections. Forgiveness, as Christ forgave us, is an act of love that enables couples to move beyond hurtful moments and strengthen their bond.

Seeking Professional Help

Sometimes, the trials faced by couples are complex and deeply rooted. In such cases, seeking professional guidance, whether from a counselor or therapist, is a wise and courageous choice. Christian counseling, in particular, can provide couples with a faith-based perspective on their issues and help them find solutions in alignment with their beliefs.

Counseling is not a sign of weakness but a demonstration of a commitment to the marriage. It can be a powerful tool for healing and growth, allowing couples to navigate challenges and emerge stronger on the other side.

Growing Through Trials

In "Marriage Matters: Christian Wisdom for Couples," we explore the idea that facing challenges in marriage is an opportunity for growth. Challenges test the depth of love, the strength of faith, and the power of forgiveness. By navigating these trials together, couples can emerge with a deeper bond and a greater understanding of the love that mirrors Christ's love for His Church.

As you continue your journey through the challenges and joys of Christian marriage, may you remember that faith, patience, and forgiveness can transform adversity into a stepping stone toward a stronger, more resilient relationship. "Navigating Challenges Together" is not just a chapter title but a testament to the enduring nature of your love and commitment as a couple.

7

A Life of Purpose

Marriage Matters: Christian Wisdom for Couples

In the quiet moments of their lives, as the evening sun cast a warm and gentle glow upon their home, Sarah and Michael found themselves reflecting on the purpose that had unfolded throughout their journey of Christian marriage. In this chapter, "A Life of Purpose," we explore the profound impact that faith and Christian wisdom can have on the lives of married couples, as they seek to live a life that aligns with God's plan.

The Purpose of Christian Marriage

A Christian marriage is not merely a partnership for companionship; it is a sacred covenant with a divinely ordained purpose. It is a union designed to reflect the love of Christ for His Church, to raise godly offspring, and to support one another in the pursuit of holiness. The purpose of Christian marriage is to walk together in faith, growing closer to God as a couple, and inviting others to experience His love through their love for each other.

As couples strive to understand and live out this purpose, they find deeper meaning and fulfillment in their marital journey.

Serving Together in Ministry

One of the ways couples can infuse purpose into their marriage is by serving together in ministry. Engaging in acts of service and outreach to the community and the church not only fulfills a call to love and serve but also strengthens the marital bond. It provides a sense of shared purpose as couples use their unique gifts and talents to make a positive impact on the world.

Christian service reminds couples that their love is not meant to be kept within the confines of their relationship but is a powerful force that can inspire and transform the lives of others. It exemplifies the love and service that Christ showed during His earthly ministry.

Nurturing Spiritual Growth

A life of purpose in a Christian marriage also includes the ongoing commitment to nurture spiritual growth. This involves regular prayer, Bible study, and participation in church activities. By making spirituality a central aspect of their lives, couples continually draw closer to God and each other.

The spiritual growth of each individual contributes to the collective growth of the marriage. As couples deepen their understanding of God's wisdom and seek to live out His principles, their love becomes more profound and their shared purpose more pronounced.

A Source of Inspiration to Others

A life of purpose in a Christian marriage becomes a source of inspiration to others. When others see a couple who loves, serves, and lives out their faith together, it serves as a beacon of hope. It showcases the transformative power of God's love in human lives and provides an example for others to follow.

In this way, the purpose-driven Christian marriage becomes a testament to God's love, spreading His message of hope, love, and salvation to the world.

The Journey Continues

"A Life of Purpose" is not just a chapter title but a call to action for couples embarking on the journey of "Marriage Matters: Christian Wisdom for Couples." The purpose of Christian marriage is a continual pursuit, an ongoing adventure of love, faith, and service. It is a commitment to live a life that reflects God's love and grace.

As you continue to explore the depths of your own Christian marriage, may you find meaning, fulfillment, and a sense of divine purpose. In your love and commitment to each other, may you illuminate the path for others to discover the profound beauty of a life centered on faith and the purpose that marriage can bring.

8

Cherishing the Journey

Marriage Matters: Christian Wisdom for Couples

In the warmth of their shared moments, Sarah and Michael realized that their journey through Christian marriage was not only a path of trials and triumphs but a beautiful tapestry of shared experiences, deepened love, and growing faith. In this chapter, "Cherishing the Journey," we delve into the importance of reflection and appreciation in a Christian marriage and how embracing the journey itself becomes a profound source of wisdom and spiritual growth.

Reflection and Gratitude

Christian wisdom encourages couples to reflect on the path they have traveled together. It's a time to pause and take stock of the lessons learned, the love shared, and the growth that has taken place. Gratitude for the journey, with all its ups and downs, becomes a cornerstone of a thriving Christian marriage.

In Colossians 3:15-17, the Bible calls for thankfulness, saying, "Let the peace of Christ rule in your hearts, since as members of one body you were called to peace. And be thankful." Gratitude for the journey serves as a reminder of

God's grace and blessings in the marriage.

The Beauty of Milestones

Milestones, whether they are anniversaries, birthdays, or significant life events, provide an opportunity for couples to celebrate their journey. It's a time to reflect on the years together, the growth as individuals and as a couple, and the shared moments that have enriched their love.

These milestones can be celebrated with prayer, thanksgiving, and expressions of love. They serve as markers of the faithfulness of God and the enduring love that has carried the couple through the years.

Lessons from the Journey

Every step in a Christian marriage journey offers valuable lessons. The trials teach resilience and patience, while the joyful moments remind couples of the importance of gratitude and the power of love. The journey itself is a classroom where couples learn to trust, forgive, and grow.

Sharing these lessons with each other and with others in their faith community is a way for couples to bear witness to the transformative power of a Christ-centered marriage. Their journey becomes a source of wisdom and guidance for those who follow.

Strengthening the Bond Through Reflection

Reflection on the journey is not merely about looking back but about strengthening the bond for the future. As couples reflect on their shared experiences, they can identify areas of growth and improvement, set new goals, and renew their commitment to the Christian marriage covenant.

By taking the time to cherish the journey, couples deepen their love and reinforce their shared faith. This practice helps keep the marriage vibrant and continues to build on the wisdom gained over the years.

Embracing the Journey Ahead

In "Cherishing the Journey," we find that the Christian marriage journey is not static; it is continually evolving. By reflecting on the past, cherishing the present, and looking ahead to the future, couples create a roadmap for continued growth and spiritual enrichment.

As you continue your own journey through Christian marriage, may you find joy and wisdom in cherishing the path you've walked together. In the warmth of gratitude, the beauty of milestones, and the lessons from the journey, may your love deepen and your faith continue to flourish. Cherishing the journey is not the end; it's an ongoing practice that keeps your marriage vibrant and enduring.

9

Sustaining Hope

Marriage Matters: Christian Wisdom for Couples

In the ever-evolving tapestry of their lives, Sarah and Michael had faced moments of uncertainty, but the thread of hope had remained steadfast, weaving itself into the very fabric of their Christian marriage. In this chapter, "Sustaining Hope," we delve into the significance of hope as an anchor for couples facing challenges and the ways in which Christian wisdom guides them in maintaining hope in the face of adversity.

The Biblical Foundation of Hope

Christian faith rests upon a foundation of hope. In Hebrews 11:1, we find a fundamental definition of faith: "Now faith is confidence in what we hope for and assurance about what we do not see." Hope is an integral component of faith, and it is this hope that sustains Christian couples through the trials they encounter.

Hope is the assurance that God is in control and that His promises will be fulfilled. This certainty is what empowers couples to face difficulties with resilience and unwavering trust.

Hope in the Face of Trials

Christian marriages are not immune to difficulties, but they are built upon the bedrock of hope. When challenges arise, couples are encouraged to place their hope in God's faithfulness and in the enduring love they have for each other.

1 Peter 1:6-7 speaks directly to the role of hope in trials: "In all this you greatly rejoice, though now for a little while you may have had to suffer grief in all kinds of trials. These have come so that the proven genuineness of your faith… may result in praise, glory, and honor when Jesus Christ is revealed."

Hope serves as a beacon of light, guiding couples through the darkest of times, reminding them that, like the dawning of a new day, the trials they face will eventually give way to joy and triumph.

Prayer and Trust in God's Plan

Prayer is a vital practice for sustaining hope in a Christian marriage. It is a way for couples to pour out their hearts to God, to seek His guidance, and to find comfort in His presence. Through prayer, couples are able to release their anxieties and burdens, placing their trust in God's divine plan.

The Bible reassures believers in Jeremiah 29:11, saying, "For I know the plans I have for you, declares the Lord, plans for welfare and not for evil, to give you a future and a hope." This promise of hope is a source of strength in challenging times.

Support from the Christian Community

Christian couples do not navigate the storms of life alone. They are part of a larger community of faith that stands ready to offer support and encouragement. The Christian community provides a network of relationships that can be a source of hope and a reminder that they are not alone in their journey.

Galatians 6:2 emphasizes the role of the Christian community: "Bear one another's burdens, and so fulfill the law of Christ." When couples allow their faith community to share in their challenges and triumphs, they strengthen the bonds of hope.

Perseverance and Resilience

Sustaining hope in a Christian marriage is not a passive endeavor but one of active perseverance and resilience. Christian wisdom teaches that, despite the trials and tribulations, hope is the anchor that keeps the marriage grounded. It is the confidence that, no matter the circumstances, God's love and faithfulness endure.

As you continue to explore the depths of "Marriage Matters: Christian Wisdom for Couples," may you find strength and courage in sustaining hope. In the embrace of hope, you discover the capacity to weather life's storms, to find joy in adversity, and to nurture a love that endures. Hope is not just a concept but a powerful force that anchors your marriage in the unchanging love of Christ.

10

The Legacy of Love

Marriage Matters: Christian Wisdom for Couples

As Sarah and Michael looked back on the journey of their Christian marriage, they realized that they were not only living out their love story but also crafting a legacy of love that would continue to impact their family, their community, and their faith for generations to come. In this final chapter, "The Legacy of Love," we explore the profound significance of leaving behind a legacy of love and how Christian wisdom plays a pivotal role in this process.

The Enduring Impact of Love

A Christian marriage, grounded in love and faith, extends far beyond the individuals involved. It creates ripples that touch the lives of family, friends, and even strangers. The legacy of love is the mark that a couple leaves on the world, a testament to the enduring nature of God's love.

The impact of love is not limited to the present but extends into the future. Children raised in a home filled with love and faith often carry these values into their own lives and relationships, continuing the legacy of love.

Passing on Faith and Values

Central to the legacy of love is the transmission of faith and values to the next generation. Christian couples are entrusted with the responsibility of nurturing a love for God and a deep understanding of Christian principles in their children. This involves teaching, modeling, and practicing faith in daily life.

Deuteronomy 6:7 emphasizes this responsibility: "Impress them on your children. Talk about them when you sit at home and when you walk along the road, when you lie down and when you get up." The legacy of love is not solely about passing down material possessions but about instilling a deep and enduring faith in the hearts of one's descendants.

Serving and Witnessing Together

The legacy of love is also manifested through a couple's service to their community and their witness of Christ's love. Christian couples who serve together in ministry, outreach, and acts of compassion demonstrate the transformative power of faith in action. By serving as a united front, they inspire others and become living examples of God's love.

In this way, the legacy of love extends beyond the family unit and reaches those who witness the couple's commitment to their faith and to each other.

Honoring the Marriage Covenant

Christian wisdom teaches that honoring the marriage covenant is an essential aspect of the legacy of love. By living out the principles of love, respect, and faithfulness, a couple exemplifies the divine relationship between Christ and His Church.

In a world where the sanctity of marriage is often challenged, couples who honor their covenant provide a powerful witness of God's design for love and commitment. Their legacy becomes a testament to the enduring nature of love in the face of cultural changes and challenges.

The Continuation of the Journey

As we conclude the journey through "Marriage Matters: Christian Wisdom for Couples," it's important to recognize that the legacy of love is not an endpoint but a continuation of the journey. It is a call to live out one's faith and love with intention, knowing that the impact will reach far beyond the couple themselves.

May your own legacy of love be one that inspires, nurtures faith, and serves as a beacon of hope to those who follow. In the enduring love and wisdom of Christ, may your marriage leave a mark on the world that reflects the profound love of God and the transformative power of faith.

11

Book Summary: Marriage Matters: Christian Wisdom for Couples

"Marriage Matters: Christian Wisdom for Couples" is a deeply insightful and spiritually enriching guide that explores the profound connection between Christian faith and the institution of marriage. This book, a beacon of wisdom and guidance, takes readers on a transformative journey through the various facets of Christian marriage, offering practical advice, profound insights, and spiritual principles that strengthen the marital bond.

The book consists of ten enlightening chapters, each delving into a critical aspect of Christian marriage, from understanding the divine nature of the marital covenant to nurturing emotional and physical intimacy. It emphasizes that love is not just a sentiment but a choice, a reflection of the selfless love modeled by Christ for His Church.

Chapter 1, "The Divine Covenant," sets the tone by highlighting the sacred foundation of Christian marriage, emphasizing its divine nature and the profound covenant it forms between two souls. The subsequent chapters explore vital components of a thriving Christian marriage, including love as a daily action, the art of communication, the sanctity of intimacy, family and faith, navigating challenges, cherishing the journey, and sustaining hope.

The book underscores the significance of hope as an anchor for couples facing adversity and the power of prayer and trust in God's plan. It encourages couples to seek support from the Christian community and actively persevere through trials.

"Marriage Matters" also sheds light on the legacy of love that couples craft through their faith-filled journey. It emphasizes the enduring impact of love, the transmission of faith and values to the next generation, serving and witnessing together, and honoring the marriage covenant as critical elements of this legacy.

In conclusion, "Marriage Matters: Christian Wisdom for Couples" is a profound resource that invites couples to deepen their understanding of the divine wisdom that underpins Christian marriage. By combining faith with practical wisdom, this book equips couples with the tools needed to create a resilient, loving, and faith-filled partnership that not only enriches their own lives but also serves as a beacon of hope, love, and faith to those around them. It is a testament to the enduring nature of love and the transformative power of faith within the sacred institution of marriage.

www.ingramcontent.com/pod-product-compliance
Lightning Source LLC
LaVergne TN
LVHW020500080526
838202LV00057B/6076